Variations on Normal

Variations on Normal

Dominic Wilcox

Square Peg

I've convinced myself that inside every single thing in the world there are hundreds of surprising ideas, connections and possibilities waiting to be discovered. I just need to look closer to find them.

Some of the ideas in this book came to me while I was in the bath or sitting on the bus or eating a sandwich or watching a hedgehog.

Dominic Wilcox

The Ages of Modern Man

Toothbrush/Maraca

Queue Head rest

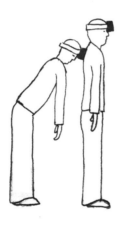

Cushion

Genetically modified square peas
to stop rolling around on plate
for easier eating.

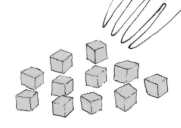

Secret snack area

A door book

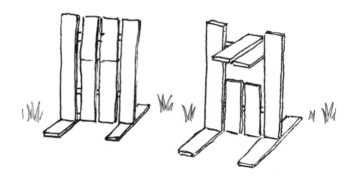

Sitting on the fence seat

Hairdryer

How to weigh a cloud

Genetically Modified Fish
For easier Fishing.

High rise building disguised as grassy hill.

Random
telephone

Sideways Trampoline

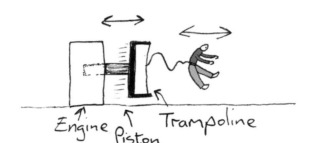

Engine

Piston

Trampoline

Space saving
Elastic measuring tape

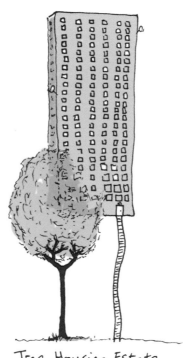

Tree Housing Estate

Remote control Sun Shade

24 hour Person

Two people are strapped
together. One sleeps while
the other goes about normal
life. The awake person notes
down what he/she has done
so that, when the sleeping
person wakes up, they can swap
over and continue.

Autumn Olympics:

Windy walking challenge

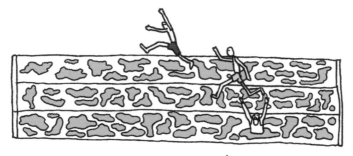

Deep puddle avoiding race

Ship
Port

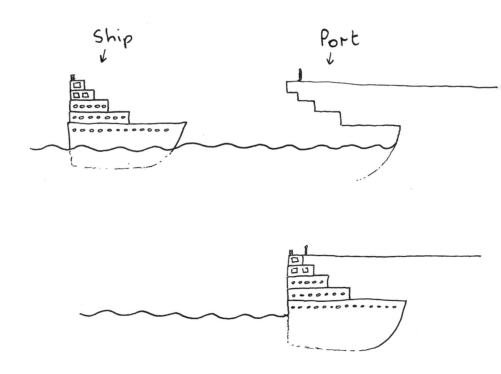

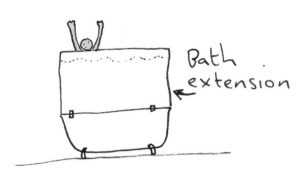

Bath
extension

Disciplining Lawbreakers

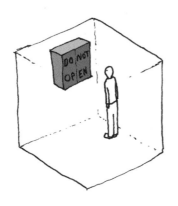

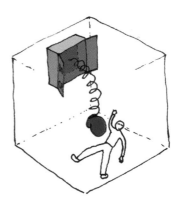

① Place lawbreaker in room

② wait

Lecture accessories

Ringtone detecting
telephone blaster

Apparatus for vertical sleeping.

Football stud

Secret
place
for a sweet

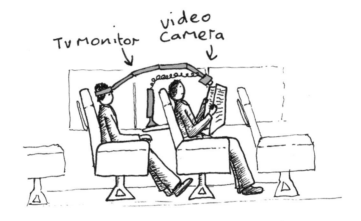

TV monitor

video camera

Unsubtle device for reading a
fellow passenger's newspaper.

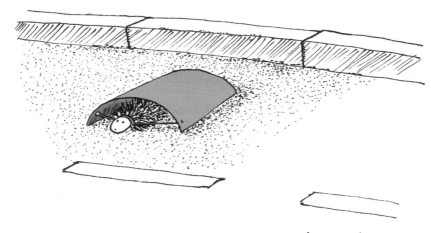

Hedgehog Road Crossing Protection Device

Personal Canned Laughter

Makes your terrible jokes seem hilarious

Pots →

Umbrella with inbuilt plant pots.
keep dry and water your flowers.

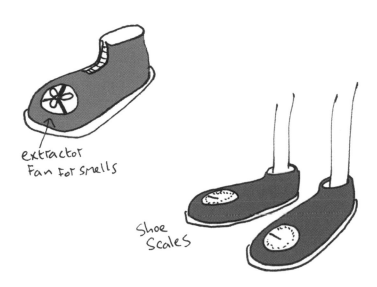

extractor
Fan for smells

Shoe
Scales

Spread out while satisfying your partner's need for a cuddle

Soft breath
Simulation

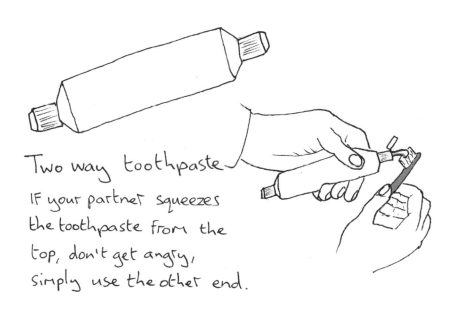

Two way toothpaste

IF your partner squeezes
the toothpaste from the
top, don't get angry,
simply use the other end.

screw-hole

screw

A screw-in shoe table

Automatic
tipping
cup

Tip
Button

Make use of your
sneezing with this
wearable ornamental
windmill.

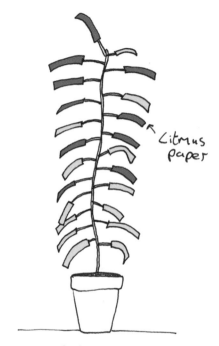

Litmus
paper

Beautiful Litmus Plant
Turns a lovely red in acid rain

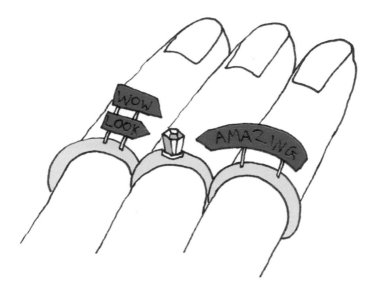

Side signage rings to bring more attention to your engagement ring.

Yo-Yo
Bungee

Nose Holes to cover

A = 0 1 2
G = 0 1 2 3
C* = 0 2
D* = 2

0 = left nostril

Musical Nose Job

Three holes are made
in the nasal passage.

Scarf with internal
propeller engine.

Skis made of ice
for street use.

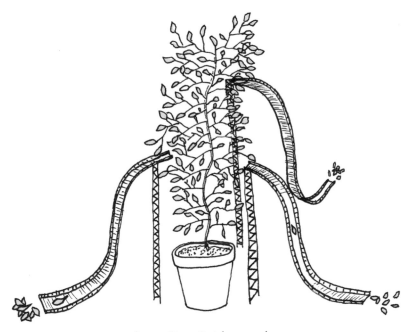

Slides for falling leaves

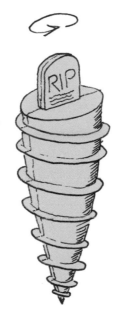

Screw-in
coffins

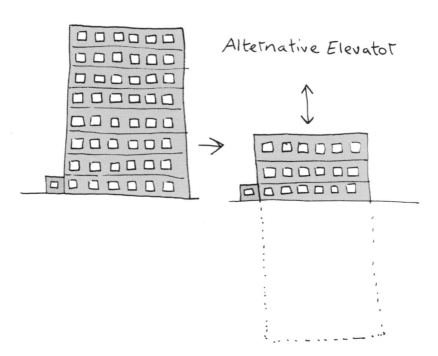

Alternative Elevator

Suitcase with robotic legs.
No more dragging your case around.

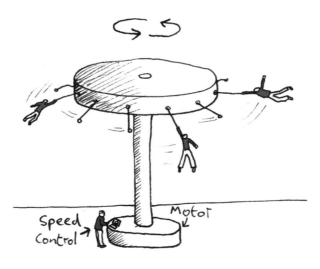

Speed Control →

Motor

Machine to strengthen
the grip of those with
a weak handshake.

Snoring Solution

The snorer is woken up
immediately by their own
microphoned snoring noise

← Headphones
set to Maximum
Volume

↑
microphone

Fly down warning device

Personal space
accessory

note:
Possible issue of
excessive distance
if two people wearing
the device meet.

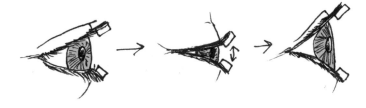

Eyelash attachments
using two repelling magnets
of the same polarity to
stop audience members
falling asleep.

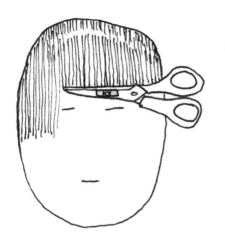

Spirit Level for perfectly horizontal haircuts

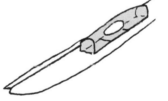

What they do with
the cut out colander holes.

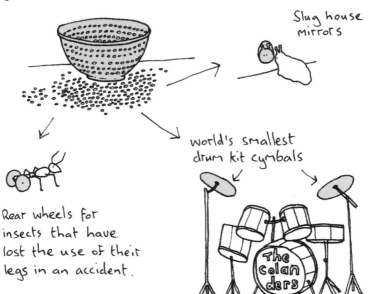

Slug house
mirrors

Rear wheels for
insects that have
lost the use of their
legs in an accident.

world's smallest
drum kit cymbals

The
colan
ders

Climbing Wall Kitchen Design

For weight loss and healthy living

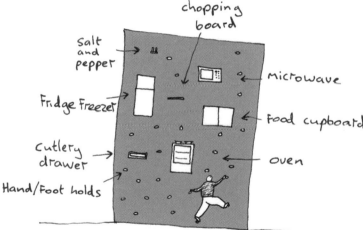

salt and pepper

chopping board

microwave

Fridge Freezer

Food cupboard

cutlery drawer

oven

Hand/Foot holds

Giant Frisbee Transport

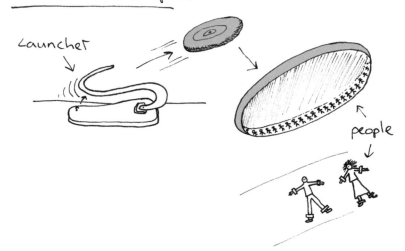

Launcher

people

Lose dirt and find muscles.

Sponge weight lifting wrist Bands

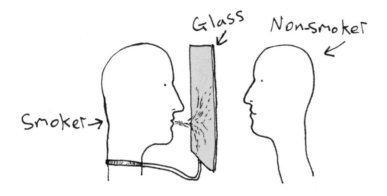

A device to enable non-smokers to talk to smokers.

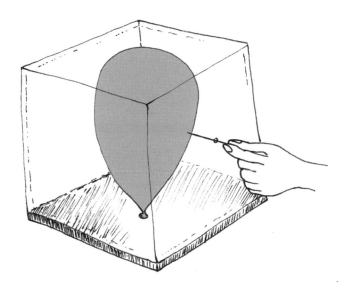

Sound Proof Balloon Popping Box

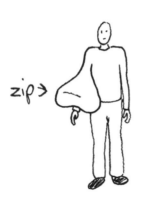

zip →

Sleeve
Bag

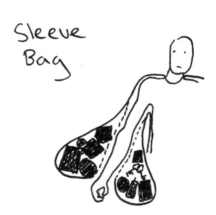

Eyebrow clip spectacles

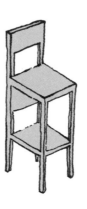

Bunk Chair

Ball kick Smoothie Maker

Hot air balloon
with side basket

Cloud sucker

Cloud water Converter

Bird class seat

walk forwards but move backwards

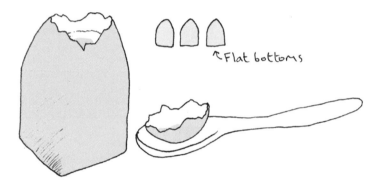

↖Flat bottoms

Genetically modified egg (cup)

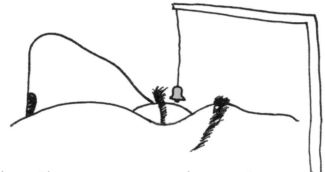

when the eyes open the eyelashes
hit the bell, which rings to indicate
that the sleeping person has woken up.

Family Poncho

vertical queue

Queue jumper

Punishment for queue jumpers

Make use of the person in front.
Handy for drinks and snacks.

Queue
Shoulder
Hook
Table

Uses for a teleporter in the home

① Replacing toilet roll

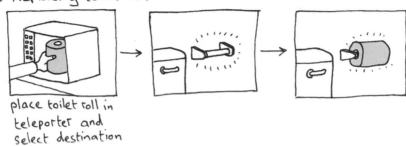

place toilet roll in
teleporter and
select destination

② Change TV channel

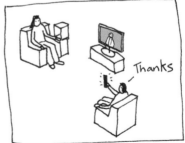

The 'Hug Bug'

← or →

Drive in either direction while hugging

on/off switch↗

Tea cup and saucer
with built in cooling fan.
(no more burnt tongues)

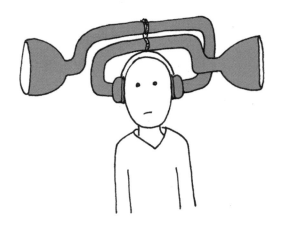

Reverse Listening Device.

Hear sounds on your right,
through your left ear
and vice versa.

Dual use coffin/workdesk

Ideal for those who work hard
all their lives and then die.

salty thumb lolly

Electric

Dodgem Roller Skates

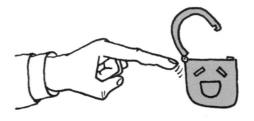

A lock that can only
be opened by tickling

Cost saving 5 plank Fence

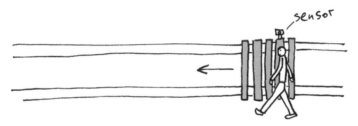

sensor detects position of person
and moves fence accordingly

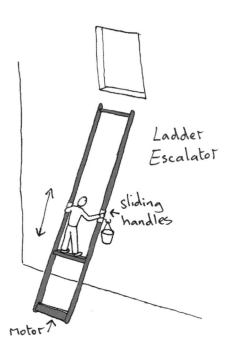

Ladder
Escalator

sliding
handles

Motor ↑

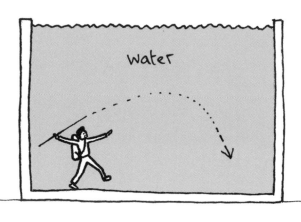

water

Javelin practice in confined places

Personal Head Airbag

① ②

Fly Swat
Eyelash Extensions

2nd Brain

Wig with built-in camera and microphone to act as a memory back-up.

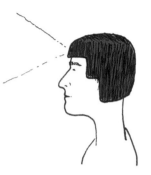

Camera

Mini computer
Hard drive

Microphone

How to appear to make eye contact whilst also accurately touching glasses when toasting each other.

One way mirror

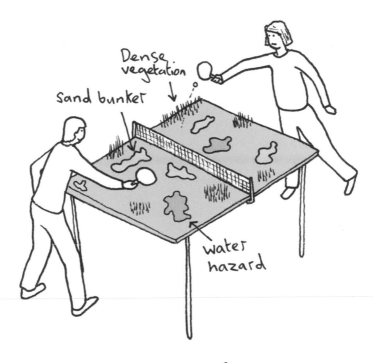

Dense vegetation

sand bunker

water hazard

Golf Ping Pong

Get away from it all.

For those who wish to go somewhere and just stick their head in the ground.

A specially designed head hole with air pipe.

The three stages of relationships

Family
Bean Bag

Portable Bottom Seat

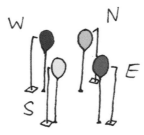

Wind Direction Device

A balloon pops on a pin
when the wind blows,
therefore revealing the
wind direction.

Tear-off
tablecloth

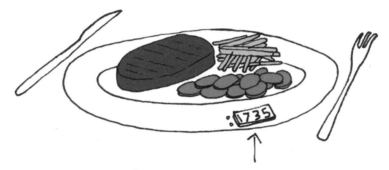

Plate that keeps count of the
number of meals eaten upon it.

Clip-on
Radio controlled
mechanical leg
movement aid
for the lazy.

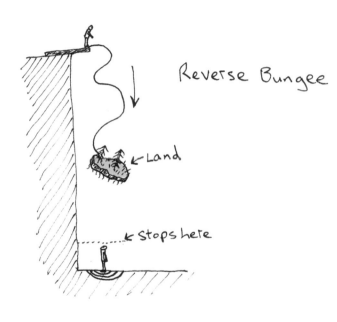

Reverse Bungee

Land

Stops here

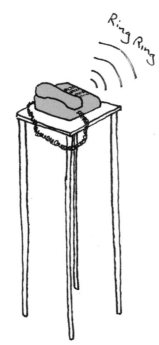

Ring Ring

Reverse Telephone

A telephone that constantly
rings until someone calls.
Then it falls silent.

Sick Bag Beard

Sick bag →

← False beard

Be sick without attracting the public's attention.

Man being sick on bus.

water

Motor

Mist spray
From tubes

Fog dress

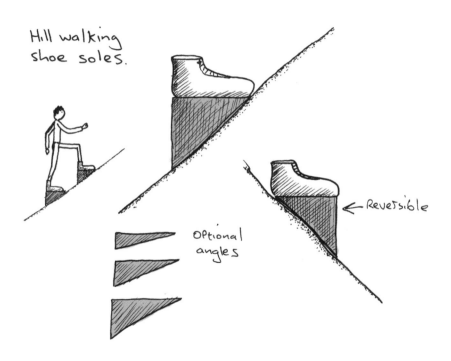

Hill walking shoe soles.

Optional angles

← Reversible

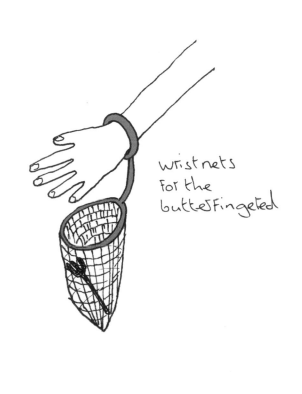

wrist nets
for the
butterfingered

On/off

suction motor

Drinking straw
suction adapter.
For those who
don't wish to waste
their energy sucking.

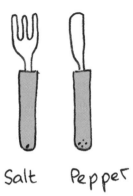

Salt   Pepper

A bicycle that loses
weight as you cycle

Insulting Ball

Encourages youngsters to kick it and therefore improve their skills.

Vote rigging avoidance method

The voters stick their vote directly onto the politician of their choice. Thus the winner is clearly seen.

Bottle attachments to allow more
sophisticated drinking out of the bottle

A chair slide.
Making the act
of sitting down
even more enjoyable.

Live Video Dating

For men who find it easier to talk to women on an LCD screen.

Punishment for litterers

propeller

motor ↗

Indoor Flag

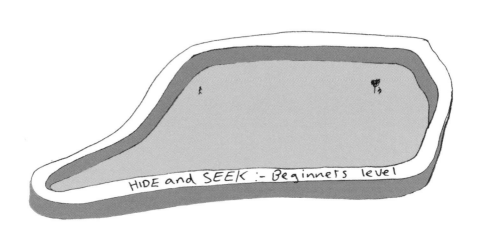

HIDE and SEEK :- Beginners level

Flood defence Objects

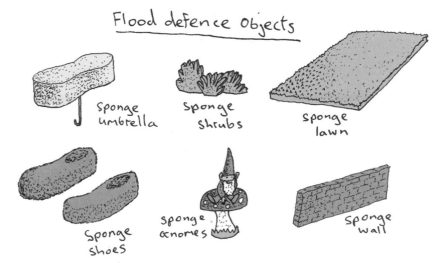

Sponge
umbrella

Sponge
Shrubs

sponge
lawn

Sponge
Shoes

sponge
Gnomes

Sponge
wall

WaterFall Umbrella

Piggyback seat

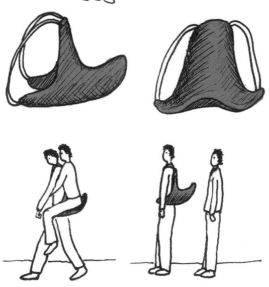

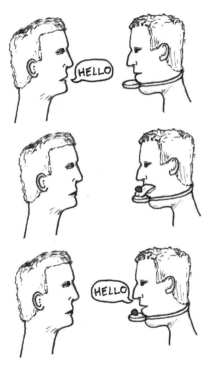

Don't speak with your mouth full.

Name GPS

For those who forget
names in social situations

"You are facing 'Tom'
turn left to face
'Clare'."

Cloud Catcher

First published in Great Britain by Square Peg 2014

2 4 6 8 10 9 7 5 3

Square Peg
Random House, 20 Vauxhall Bridge Road,
London SW1V 2SA

www.vintage-books.co.uk

Addresses for companies within The Random House Group Limited
can be found at www.randomhouse.co.uk/offices.htm

The Random House Group Limited Reg. No 954009

A CIP catalogue record for this book available from the British Library

ISBN 9780224098878

Printed and bound in Italy by
L.E.G.O. S.p.A.

British artist, designer and inventor Dominic Wilcox lived a perfectly normal life in the north east of England until the age of 19. Since then he has read the dictionary, twice, battled against a 3D printer at the V&A Museum and shown his odd, surprising and thought-provoking designs at galleries around the world.

After graduating from the Royal College of Art in London he set about creating things that made him feel happy, excited and intrigued. His innovative work has become known internationally for its playful and understated style, regularly solving problems people hadn't previously realised they had.

Notable works include: 'No Place Like Home' GPS shoes that guide the wearer to their desired destination, and miniature sculptures balanced on the moving hands of watches.

Website: dominicwilcox.com
Blog: variationsonnormal.com
Twitter: @dominicwilcox